This book is dedicated to my wife Cindy who furnished the title and undertook the difficult task of proof reading the original manuscript.

The Art of Dying

Transforming the Fear of Death

"In Joy we are Created,
In Joy we are Sustained,
into Joy we will Depart"
                    -The Upanishads

'The King's Chamber' *by Manly P. Hall.*

- Front Cover- "St. Veronica's handkerchief" by Gabe Von Max
- Back Cover- "Stairway to Heaven" by Jim Warren

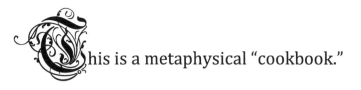

This is a metaphysical "cookbook."

For those already sitting at the Feast of Truth there is no need for such recipes. They are fortunate enough to come to Faith naturally. Others require an intellectual map in order to find their way to the Banquet Table. Fortunately enlightenment doesn't care how you get there.

Most of us agree that humanity stands at the threshold of unspeakable change and can feel clouds of despair eclipsing the spirit. Hopefully, those longing for the Light at the end of the tunnel will find the information as helpful as it was for me.

It deals with spiritual principles and 'devices' but it's not a religious essay. It operates on the assumption that "God is too big to fit inside any one religion."

I really had little to do with it, except to ask questions and write down the answers. The wisdom comes from my teacher and guide Ariel (See Appendix D) but the source is not as important as the information. Nor do I understand it all myself. I am just as inspired by this information as any student in search of that coveted AH-HA! moment!

The mildly curious or those with poor attention span may not find it to their liking. For this reason I have abandoned any attempt to 'dumb it down' or rewrite it in order to make it more palatable to the unmotivated.

It's up to the reader to contemplate and connect the dots. Spiritually, this may be seen as the western equivalent of Jnana Yoga, the path of Wisdom. It is *occult* rather than mystical and *conceptual* rather than emotional. Those who climb the Mountain of Truth via this path of *Knowledge* may find these instructions offer a rapid (but *steep)* path up the Cone of

Consciousness. May Love and Light guide us all until we join at that Apex of *Perfect Peace Profound.* –R

Contents

Dying the Good Death

*"There are those who do not realize that one day we all must die.
Those who realize this, swiftly settle their quarrels. – Buddha*

riel, as a child, when I learned that we all eventually die, I would wake up at night terrified of losing my parents. Later this fear grew to include my own Life. Fear of death is universal isn't it?

A: You have no idea how all pervasive the fear of death is. That is why dealing with this problem is the highest priority for those of us whose job it is to help the life forms on Earth.

R: I would like to die a good death but I don't fear it. I resist the idea of suffering, however.

A: You don't *consciously* fear death. But in denial, this fear is alive and well. All suffering appears when you resist change. Death is the ultimate change and hence your ultimate fear. The fear of death sits on the throne of your discomfort.

R: *All* suffering is rooted in the fear of death?

A: Yes, all suffering. Change comes like waves from the invisible world and to know Joy, you must learn to surf them instead of being pounded by them.

R: I think a lot of my fear of death comes from the nuns involved with my Catholic upbringing. They would slap their Bibles with a ruler and threaten, *"The fearful shall have their part in the lake which burneth."* which is enough to scare the hell out of you.

A: More accurately, it can scare the hell INTO you. This fear is a prime example of a circular 'ring-pass-not.' (See Page 43) **You can become *frightened of being frightened and even this becomes frightening*. Circular thoughts like this would go on forever if you didn't have help breaking free of them.**

R: And fortunately that's where you come in.

A: Everyone needs assistance from forces larger than themselves. When you are finally helped off that vicious fear circle, your wish of "dying the good death" won't even be an issue. *In fact you won't experience death at all*.

R: I'm for that.

A: It's my job to help create the point of view that allows this to happen. Learning the right attitude to hold at the moment of crossing over is all important to "dying the good death".

Attaining the 'Beginner's Mind'

In the beginner's mind there are many possibilities.
In the expert's mind there are few. – Suzuki

hat IS the right frame of mind for a dying person?

A: The best mental state for dying is *Grateful expectancy*. But first you have to eliminate those denied fear circles first. You can't have spiritual blockages and be able to do this fully.

R: There's that old adage again, "Gratitude is the greatest attitude."

A: Gratitude is the Song of the Universe. It is a river of intense and ecstatic vibration bridging the very highest parts of Creation with the lowest. Choirs of Angels actually sing huge waves of Gratitude into existence for all to enjoy and get healed by. The miraculous thing about Gratitude is that it blesses the giver as much as the receiver.

R: Is Gratitude an antidote to fear?

A: The very best and it accelerates your growth exponentially. It is not possible for the ego to exist in the presence of Gratitude. Such an "antidote" allows your consciousness to expand into Joy without hesitation.

R: I know people who are totally unfamiliar with Gratitude. Is Joy not possible for them?

A: Sooner or later, Joy is the final resting state for everyone. All it requires is a little willingness to practice.

R: What kind of practice?

A: Get in the habit of looking up to the sky and generating a little thankfulness for the many good things in your life. By doing this, you stimulate the Heavens which in turn, get the seed of Gratitude germinating in *you*.

R: Who would an atheist be grateful to?

A: Most westerners have been told, "only God is worthy of Gratitude." But Gratitude doesn't need to be directed anywhere in particular. Gratefulness <u>is its own reward</u>!

R: And just sending it upward and outward is sufficient?

A: Yes. Gratitude will bless myriads of beings as well as yourself without you ever being aware of it. It will even make Nature itself more radiant. <u>A person fortunate enough to die in a state of Gratitude will find harmonic resonance with choirs of angelic beings and be instantly transported to the Crown of Consciousness!</u>

R: That is a promising goal but constant Gratitude is hard to maintain.

A: You have always wanted to learn a second language. Why not study the language Heaven? Before your departure into the Far Country wouldn't it be great if you could converse freely with its inhabitants? When it comes to "foreign" dialects, Gratitude, the language of Angels is golden.

Only One Problem

hy do humans seem beset with so very many problems these days?

A: The fact that they *think* they have so many problems IS the problem. As we have discussed, people really have only one problem and that is the FEAR OF DEATH! ALL fears are rooted in this one *single* fear. *Humans spend their whole life running from this shadow of fear.*

Running from "the devil" she sees in her own shadow.

R: Well, most people seem scared about many things, like not having enough money, terrorists, geopolitics, poor health, etc. It seems like there is an abundance of different kinds of fear out there.

A: The fear of death has many masks but only one face.

R: Fear seems to underline almost everything. It's probably worse now, thanks to the internet and the age of instant information.

A: Yes, fear is contagious and instant global networking has allowed it to grip the hearts of humanity like a single fist closing around the throat of a frightened child. Humanity is laboring beneath a sense of inevitable and impending doom. You keep it in denial, pushed back and out of sight where it festers. If your 360 degree vision was operating properly, you would see that death is but a shadow cast by your ego.

R: If the fear of death is in denial and out of our field of vision, how can we deal with it? Doesn't fear have to be confronted in order to be eliminated?

A: It can't be eliminated but there are psychological devices that can coax it out of denial so that the fear of death can be transformed.

R: Transformed? Transformed into what?"

A: It is transformed into its opposite, which of course is Love.

R: I thought the opposite of fear is Faith?

A: That is true also. Faith leads to Knowledge and Knowledge leads to Love. Consider fear as a 'battery' that has been put in an appliance backward and is creating a short circuit. You don't want to throw the battery away, but simply reverse the polarity. This allows you, as an "appliance of consciousness," to be filled with your native divine essence.

R: I'm familiar with many of your 'devices' from our earlier interviews. Do you have a device for understanding and transforming fear?

A: Any device I might give you would require a couple of necessary observations which can't be stated too often:

1. _All fear has a singular cause, and that is the belief in the possibility of death._

2. _Humans use denial to protect themselves from having to face this debilitating terror._

This terror exists in the lower planes of existence. Even physical pain is simply the fear of death on a cellular level.

R: Do you mean the cells in my body experience fear?

A: That's correct and you experience this as physical pain.

R: Since it's obvious that joy depends upon dealing with this fear, why do we resist it so much?

A: It is because you _believe that death is real_.

R: If death isn't real, then what is it?

A: Death is simply an idea, albeit a BAD idea. It's a bad idea because it isn't true.

R: Well, babies don't worry about death do they?

A: Neither do your pets. But that dark shadow stalks most sentient humans like a wraith from the first moment they embraced the idea.

R: So if it is just an idea why don't we simply just forget about it?

A: **Unfortunately, this viral intruder is now so entangled into your global thought system that it usually stays with most people until their death bed where it is transformed by the mandatory stage of *acceptance*.** (See Appendix A)

Transcending the Grand Illusion
Celebrating the death of Death

"My dear Krishna, O infallible one, my illusion *is now gone. I have regained my memory"* - Arjuna

ow do we talk ourselves out of believing death is real? It seems impossible when we see things falling apart and dying around us. It certainly seems real when we see our loved ones die.

A: **This information is deep and difficult to accept for many but the truth is, *all your loved ones who have died have never been more alive than they are right now!* Since you have constructed your current world with images from the past, these memories are all you see projected upon your movie screen of Creation. If you could learn to release your past you would release death itself to shrink back into its native nothingness.**

R: Well, accepting death as just an idea originating from the past is hard for the loved ones left behind.

A: How can Love be lost when all Creation is made of Love? You ask, "What about my loved ones who have passed away?" The truth is that you don't <u>have</u> any loved ones who passed away; you have MEMORIES of loved ones who passed away.

R: But I have pictures to prove they existed.

A: Now this is difficult and few will agree with it but the only thing pictures prove is that you have memories, but memories are never accurate. The past can never be proven. *Only you, NOW, in this moment can be proven.* 'I AM' simply cannot be refuted. The past on the other hand is just an *idea* that you nurture and protect, just as death is an idea you nurture and protect. You are afraid *not* to believe in death. The thought is terrifying...... but it is at least familiar.

R: "The devil you know is preferable to the devil you don't know."

A: Familiarity *seems* to help you feel more secure because it suggests that there are some things that don't change. Your family photographs don't change, that's why you like them.

R: Not believing in the past is a huge challenge.

A: Most people can't do it until they face the end of their lives. But let it be known that all the Love you have *ever* experienced in the past is available right now in this moment.

R: I suppose that's what's meant by the phrase "Love is forever?"

A: Love is forever because it is indestructible and Eternal! The fastest way to become immortal is to become Love itself.

R: I can hear the song now, "All you need is Love."

A: But in order for Love to blossom, you must remove everything that *blocks* Love within you.

R: And you say this is done by simply eliminating the belief in the past?

A: Yes, but it requires a bit of willingness to return to your Source. This seems hard because you are in the habit of accepting the past as real so you need a little diligence to re-program yourself from this dream.

R: It's true; I can't really prove the past ever happened.

A: The reason you can't prove the past ever happened is *because it didn't*. You have been partaking of a magnificent dream of dying that humans have collectively fashioned and maintained in their dungeons of denial! But you are on the threshold of finding out that you have no past. You are discovering that you are not subject to time but are "Nowness" itself.

R: So, the only thing I can really prove is 'I AM.'

A: This is your Magnum Opus. 'I AM' is *Now and nothing but Now*! You are not 'I Was,' nor 'I Will Be.' You are an ever new and ever emerging deeper version of Now. *All* else is an illusion.

R: Well, it is not easy to be centered like that with so much disintegration happening in the world.

A: From the still, silent hub of the Eternal, you see that change doesn't happen around you, but within you. Change is all there is. _**Everything is always dying on one plane and simultaneously being born on another**_.

Those who are aware enough to create a world that understands the illusory nature of death realize the 'dark shadow of demise' is just that...only a shadow.

Practicing Dying

"While I thought I was learning how to live,
I was really learning how to die." - Leonardo Da Vinci

re there any other procedures we can do to deal with this primal fear of dying?

A: Since fear screams at you like a banshee from a dungeon in your unconscious, you need to bring it up into the Light so it can be calmed by the healing breezes of spirit. This is done simply by practicing dying.

R: I find that thought of practicing dying disturbing. That doesn't seem to be a very positive thing to do.

A: Of course you find it disturbing. Your demons don't like being exposed.

R: Do you have any devices that might make this invocation easier?

A: Visualization can be very effective. Imagine yourself on your death bed surrounded by your loved ones. See yourself facing your terror and watching it transform into a sense of adventure. Practice looking at your impending death as if you were preparing for a trip to some place you have longed to visit.

R: I have trouble visualizing my death. All I can see is me lying in a casket or a clump of ashes in a Persian urn!

A: This humor of yours is an excellent place to start because it can neutralize a multitude of screeching crouchers. But go ahead and allow yourself to imagine yourself already dead and lying in a casket.

R: OK, I can see it but I don't particularly like it.

A: Can you see what you are doing here? Can you understand that it is <u>impossible to see yourself as dead?</u> No matter how hard you try you can't do it. You are always someplace above the casket doing the watching. Consciousness cannot be extinguished. Only its location can be changed. This knowledge that from the beginning, you have always been aware and always will be, is the door to your liberation. It is now up to you to make sure that your awareness is filled with Joy and not terror.

R: How about when I was anesthetized for my back operation. I was unconscious then?

A: No. You were conscious. The only thing general anesthesia took from you is your *memory* of being conscious.

16

'Germinating' a Broken Heart

"Thy heart is but a fertile seed waiting to sprout."
- Morihei Ueshiba

The hardest thing about losing a loved one for me is the heartbreak experienced by the survivors. I think my greatest concern is how my loved ones are going to react when I croak.

A: It would be so much easier if grieving loved ones could understand the function of the broken heart. A seed must break open in order for new sprouts of Life to emerge. So it is with opening the Heart center.

R: A broken heart is an open heart?

A: If it is offered up, yes. When the heart breaks open you have the choice of either opening up to larger currents of Love from the cosmos or closing down completely for a while. A broken heart will make you either *bitter or better.* I recommend the latter as it offers a fast track opportunity for a higher love. Not all seeds sprout and not all broken hearts immediately germinate. Understanding this can help your loved ones make the right choices.

R: Could my passing actually help them?

A: They will miss you but even this serves the function of pulling them up into the higher, finer frequencies of

existence with you. Keep in mind that the passing of a loved one helps the survivors face their denied fears. Humanity *converges as it ascends* and this convergence is particularly true of a departing soul and their surviving loved ones.

The Spiral Cone Converges as it Ascends.
Such is the way of Humanity.

R: Ah, "the Circle shall be unbroken."

A: You don't want to deny them the opportunity to face and transform their fears. Transforming grief to gratitude is the goal of ALL people. *The best thing you can do is simply love them .*

R: Just love them?

A: Just love them.

The Law of Compensation

"For every treasure taken from the body, a greater one is returned to the mind. For every treasure taken from the mind, a greater one is given to the soul." – A

 hear what you say but the sense of loss is still quite real for those people left behind. It's not just the loss from the death of a loved one but it is the belief that all they have to look forward to is old age, suffering and death.

A: This is just more of the same illusion. While physical disintegration seems ever more apparent as life progresses, *new doors of Awareness and Love* open as the physical life seems to recede. Life is designed to only get better as it progresses.

R: I would imagine this positive progression requires at least a little willingness to evolve toward Love and Light.

A: That goes without saying. You don't want to resist the process. *Greater Love* is only one of the gifts from the universal Law of Compensation. *Peace* is another and so is *Faith*. Ultimately you will see that not only is death an illusion but so is entropy itself.

R: Well the fact that everything falls apart is simple physics isn't it?

A: If you see things through the strictly scientific viewpoint, the laws of physics (specifically the four laws of thermodynamics) state that energy cannot be destroyed but only changed in form and appearance. <u>Since Consciousness is nothing but organized energy, it cannot be destroyed either</u>. Like water, it can change its appearance but its essence is still the same!

R: How important is our attitude in claiming these gifts of compensation?

A: You must remember that your mind is creative and *whatever you expect affects what you receive.* There are two ways of observing the River of Life as it flows by. You can either look downstream at those obsolete things drifting away or you can look upstream at those treasures flowing toward you.

R: So it is a matter of always seeing the "glass half full" rather than half empty. Some would say this is unrealistic, almost a Pollyanna *goody two shoes* type of thinking.

A: Absolute positivity is not a matter of fooling yourself or glossing over. The ultimate positive statement you can make is "I AM."

R: So *grateful expectancy* is even appropriate in this situation!

A: You have the option of beholding either your losses or your blessings. It's impossible to see both. Every moment you are called upon to judge whether you want grievance or Gratitude.

R: It's "Judgment Day!"

A: Only the 'judgment' is made by *you*, not God. In truth, it is you judging yourself and the world that surrounds you. As you judge your Life, your Life in turn judges you back in the same spirit you judged it.

R: This reflection is simply karma at work isn't it?

A: Yes. Creation is a mirror which demonstrates that you are "judged with the same judgment with which you judge." It is obviously wise to develop the habit of seeing your Life and world positively and gratefully.

Stability vs Change
The inner tension between Security and Freedom

"Life is either a daring adventure, or nothing." - Helen Keller
"Change alone is eternal, perpetual, immortal" - A. Schopenhauer
"Distrust and caution are the parents of security." - Benjamin Franklin

Which is better to ask for, freedom or security?

A: Why not both? You falsely believe you have to choose between Freedom and Security but 100% security and 100% freedom is your destiny.

R: Freedom and Security are related to gender aren't they?

A: You are correct. The Mother is usually more attracted to security for her nest, while the Father wants the freedom to go out into the world and gather resources. This duality is meant to be *complementary* and mutually reinforcing but has become a primary source of conflict in most aspects of human Life.

R: I can even see this gender thing in our American politics. The Democrats represent the Mother and her quest for Security, while the Republicans insist on Freedom and fewer government restrictions. But what does this security/freedom thing have to do with the art of dying?

A: Because the insecurity engendered by the fear of death prevents you from accepting change. You have an inner gender war going on. You must rise above this fear of losing your Security or Freedom in order for the idea of death to cease being a problem for you.

R: Is it possible that death appears *because* we refuse change?

A: Excellent! It is crucial to understand that if you cannot acknowledge the constantly moving currents of Life and insist on clinging to the unmoving shore, the shadow of death will haunt you mercilessly and your world will appear dense and impenetrable.

R: Further evidence that 'fear is creative.'

A: Humanity's insecurity and desire for safety has created a solid world where you need things like traffic lights in order to keep from bumping into each other. In the finer dimensions where Love rules, things are not so hard and dense. They can *interpenetrate*.

R: Is this interpenetration what Love is?

A: Yes, but in your world of hardened ego, Light can't penetrate your conceptual boxes. And anything that Light can't penetrate will *always* cast a shadow.

R: I get it. Solid things like religious dogma and stubborn opinions are what cast the shadow of death out into the world.

A: Exactly. Melting those frozen boxes you built out of the desire for security is the beginning of your liberation. Learning to happily surf these new liquid waves of change will allow you to recognize your own immortality.

R: In order to allow change, we need a basic faith in the goodness of the universe, don't we?

A: Faith is spiritual gold, but it must be developed and tested in order to become an established part of your being. Once that happens, you will see that there is no death but only change.

Look at the qualities of water for instance:

- **Ice *seems* to die when it changes to liquid.**
- **Water *seems* to die when it becomes steam.**
- **Steam *seems* to die when it changes into vapor, etc.**

Precisely the same transformative principles of alchemy exist between the different states of your own mind and body as well as all Spirit and Matter in Creation.

R: This stuff is really interesting but its sure challenging.

A: Spend more time in the Stillness and then you will be given the understanding. This is why the wisest among you take time to meditate and pray.

R: I usually find meditation boring.

A: At first, meditation often brings to the surface more *anxiety* than boredom. Quiet prayer and focused meditation will finally bring you to the point of recognizing that stillness is the true center of yourself and the true center of all things. But stillness isn't something to be attained; it is simply what *you are.*

R: My brain hurts. Am I supposed to embrace change or stillness? They seem diametrically opposed.

A: There is no need to do confusion here. Just realize that at the hub of Creation all things *including change* are perfectly still just like the mathematical center of a spinning wheel is perfectly still.

R: So observing change from the vantage point of stillness is the perception needed to conquer death?

A: To begin with, death can't be "conquered" because there is nothing there to conquer in the first place. What I said was, the person who understands the meaning of change won't <u>experience</u> death, even if those around him do.

R: I like that. So ultimately, death is just a viewpoint?

A: Yes, along with everything else in your existence. True spiritual adventurers see death as merely another dynamic change to be explored. It is Joy to behold Life as an eternal sequence of AWAKENINGS, forever going from one room to another exploring the many mansions of Awareness and Thought. This

joyous perception is available to anyone willing to clean out their denied terror.

Facing the "Dweller on the Threshold"

"The foreboding sign above the door proclaims:
'Abandon Hope all Ye who Enter Here.'
Terrified he enters to stare down his evil twin" - A

"I hold it true that these thoughts are living things
Endowed with bodies, breath, and wings" - Ella Wheeler Wilcox

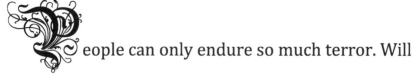eople can only endure so much terror. Will humanity ever collectively eliminate this curse and know peace?

A: Fortunately fear seems to be reaching its zenith and humanity is starting to slowly awaken. But before this awakening is complete each is called to make peace with all the terrors he or she has buried and has been unable to process earlier in Life.

R: This is what Zanoni called, "Facing the Dweller on the Threshold."

A: This is the point when *many are called but few are chosen*. The Truth of their new expanded existence is so bright and terrifying that some actually prefer the darkness of unconsciousness so as not to have to face their Dweller. It seems easier for them to retreat into denial where they must contend with their 'crouching screechers' until the gates of liberated consciousness are finally opened for them.

R: That is an intense and intimidating thought. I don't know how much garbage I have buried in me to be processed.

A: Since you are open to help from higher space, there is nothing to worry about. Anyone who simply *Wills Goodness* will glide through "fields of flowers and rooms filled with beautiful color while bathing in the enchanting Music of the Spheres."

R. That sounds really nice but I know for a fact that not all deaths are such idyllic, happy events.

A: It depends on how much preparation you have done. The very best deaths are reserved for those who sought Truth above all else because they will have awakened themselves enough to see *Birth and Death as the same event*, which in fact they are. Birth and death only *appear to be* different depending upon from which side of the veil you are looking.

R: So, what is seen as death on one side of the veil is perceived as a birth on the other?

A: Yes, while some hands are waving goodbye on one side there are welcoming hands that beckon you from the other.

Do "Heaven and Hell" Exist?

"The mind is its own place, and in itself,
can make a heaven of Hell, and a hell of Heaven. – Milton

Aren't Heaven and Hell just states of mind?

A: Everything is just a state of mind. But that doesn't make it any less profound. On every level, both individually and collectively, the Joyous state you call "Heaven" makes up your very core. The ecstasy of 'I AM' is not what humans need to become, it is *what humans are,* each and every one.

R: Ah, Heaven!

A: But the state of mind you call "hell" is more important to examine because unless it is understood, you can't totally enter those ecstatic states of bliss. While wrestling with festering, denied fear, you can't fully accept the intensely positive dynamic of your pure Existence as yet. You live in abject terror by *the possibility of becoming completely and totally yourself!*

R: And this terror is what Hell is?

A: All fear is hell. It's good to understand that suffering comes simply from resisting the ever changing flow of evolution. ("The Will of God")

R: If these changes are supposed to bring us the Joy of Heaven why do we resist them so desperately?

A: Because fear creates fire and you hate fire. You have an investment in keeping it buried and smoldering.

R: I have always associated fire with rage, not fear.

A: Rage is just a *reaction* to fear. Fear causes and generates suffering by following a cyclical progression.

1. **Fear creates resistance**
2. **Resistance creates friction.**
3. **Friction creates heat.**
4. **Too much heat creates suffering.**

R: So this is this where the so called "fires of hell" come from! I've been threatened with that since I first attended Catechism!

A: Those who teach children to fear hell fire are in danger of tasting the fiery fruits of their own threats. Like fire, fear is contagious and spreads to engulf the match that starts it.

R: I always thought that hell was just an idea created by religious leaders to manipulate their followers?

A: As long as fear exists, hell will exist. Fiery states of consciousness exist on Earth and these volatile states are generated by the fearful alone.

R: But fire isn't always bad.

A: How could it be? Fire is an Element! The metabolism in your body is a furnace after all. Fire simply needs to be balanced with the other elements, like Air and Water.

R: So then *some* fear is OK?

A: Well, *Respect* is good. So is Awe. These may be thought of as fear that has been domesticated.

R: The thought of hell itself is scary.

A: So, you are frightened!

R: I'll never admit it.

Converting 'Hell' into 'Heaven'

*"When I started counting my blessings,
my whole life turned around. "* -Willie Nelson

ren't other goals worthy of our labors, too? What about helping others?

A: The best thing a person can do to help others is to become wholly him or herself. This liberates everyone else to become wholly what they are as well. Eventually, all humanity will converge as it ascends in the perfection of Love.

R: You said that you have a device to help accomplish this.

A: Yes, one way to accomplish the liberation of unadulterated Existence is to explore the illusions of NON-existence.

R: We should explore the OPPOSITE of 'I AM?'

A: Yes, and this requires courage. The fear of the Dweller on the Threshold (the humanized form of all your collected terrors) **makes you shrink from it. But it is worth the attempt because exploring the *opposite* of your existence will reward you richly *with* Existence..**

R: The opposite of 'I AM' is 'I AM NOT,' correct?

A: Yes, but eventually you find that 'I AM NOT' is impossible. The recognition of this is the greatest gift of all. Most humans are so threatened by the foolish belief in death that they are unable to fully prove their own existence to themselves. Their default approach is to banish this fear into *denial.* When this happens the banquet feast gets thrown out before it even reaches the dinner table.

R: Doesn't denial have a positive side?

A: The purpose of denial is to act as a filter. Without denial you would be incapable of selective thinking. You need someplace to put inappropriate thoughts so you can examine your chosen thoughts individually. Without the filter of denial, all your thoughts would happen at once and you would quite literally go mad.

R: I see. The fear of death has hijacked the function of denial so it can have a handy place to hide. Amazing!

A: When that single thought of death is drawn out into the Light, the problem is automatically solved. Then there is nowhere left to go but to join your Source in orgasmic bliss with the rest of awakening humanity. This should give your choice to evolve a very high priority.

R: Since this circular fear thought is so well hidden in denial, doesn't it make examination of its contents nearly impossible?

A: It is not only possible but inevitable. Therefore liberation is inevitable. It's just a matter of how much you need to suffer before you allow your higher Self to take its rightful place on the mountain top.
(See Appendix A: The Five Stages of Grief)

Escaping your suffering requires an understanding of what has happened to humanity over the centuries. You have grown so collectively acquainted with terror that you have fashioned a living MONSTER. You collectively breathed the Breath of Life into it and proceeded to call it "The Devil."

R: I prefer the name, "Dweller on the Threshold." It is less charged and more accurate a description.

A: As you wish.

A New Heaven, a New Earth

"Aim at heaven and you get both Heaven and Earth.
Aim at earth and you get neither." - C.S. Lewis

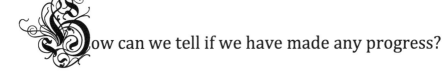

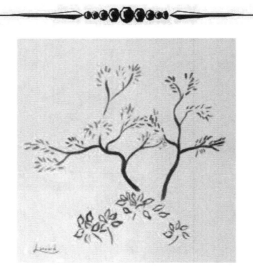

ow can we tell if we have made any progress?

A: New perceptions and new worlds start appearing when engrams (fear blockages) **are released and transformed. Some of your more enlightened friends have given the pursuit of Truth such a high priority that they stand at the door of a *magnificent birth*.**

R: The birth into the next higher dimension?

A: Yes, and this graduation to the greater expansive four dimensional existence requires awakening the

hidden vision still slumbering in the unused 90% of your brain. Many find the pursuit of Truth so troubling however that this greater vision is a gift that few are capable of handling at this time.

R: I know. Most people don't even seem interested in the topic.

A: Well, a newborn baby has no interest in learning to drive a car either, but the day will come when he or she will ask for lessons.

R: Many people don't believe in anything larger than themselves. In cases like this, *who* do they ask and *what* should they ask for?

A: They should respectfully turn their gaze outward into space and inward to their own inner world and proceed to ask the heavens: "What am I?" and "Who will I be, once awakened?" Continue to ask and the answer will accompany endless new gifts of Faith and Peace.

R: OK, now I'm asking. "What am I?" and "Who will I be once I am awakened?"

A: The answer of course, is and will always be the same, *you are Love*! You are infinite compassion adorned with spiritual eyes in the back of your head. Your Self is an infinitely caring *sphere* of loving awareness. Contrary to physical appearances you are not limited by two little eyes in a pinched little face restricted to only a 180 degree view of your world. In your awakened state you have 360 degree "surround" sight and are no longer limited to the two dimensional disk of shallow self-interest that has kept you imprisoned in Flatland for centuries!

Blowing Up Your Existential Bubble

"In all our quest of greatness, like wanton boys whose pastime's care, we follow after bubbles we have blown in the air." - John Webster

"To be or not to be, that is the question!" – Hamlet and A. Bubble

The fear of nonexistence (*not being*) is *primal* to all living things, true?

A: Of course. This is what accounts for the 'fight or flight' response from all members of the animal kingdom. If you doubt the power of this survival impulse just try to stop breathing for 5 minutes! Here

is a visual device that may help you awaken from your dream of prison.

When you blow through a soapy film you can create a bubble. The bubble is the film folded back upon itself until it is joined in the rear. Once this gap is closed, the bubble's existence is established and self-evident. It is now able to float upward to the skies, a whole new colorful and weightless spherical being.

Similarly you should be learning to allow the Breath of Spirit to inspire and inflate you into a totally aware, 'bubble' of I AM-ness with omni-directional, 360 degree Awareness!

R: I am often accused of being over inflated as it is!

A: Very humorous. The point however is this: A bubble either IS or it ISNT. There is no such thing as *half* of a bubble. Likewise, in order to become a whole entity you also must allow yourself to be fashioned into the lofty, higher state of individuality. This is your destiny. I know of no better way than this bubble analogy to help you with your birth into omni-dimensional ISNESS.

R: Is the invisible world *pulling* us or is getting to this new realm totally our own responsibility?

A: It is both. A bubble exists because its outer atmospheric pressure is equal to its inner pressure. Man's angels are drawing him Home just as I am pulling you. *But you have the responsibility of allowing me to do it.*

R: And this requires all humans to connect with their invisible guide?

A: Yes, this is the Holy Guardian Angel. (See Page 51)

R: I've always resisted that. The term HOLY Guardian Angel seems like a highly charged term. Why does it have to be "holy?" Isn't the term 'angel' good enough?

A: Why does the term "holy" make you uncomfortable? Would you prefer being guided by an unholy angel? They do exist and you must be careful not to allow them to hijack the helm of your body. You are the captain of your Being and must never abandon the wheel. Especially with the storm clouds that seem to be appearing on the horizon.

R: Understood.

A: Again, this controversial topic will be covered in depth but for most people right now, it is sufficient to *just quit creating spiritual friction by resisting the new information*. It will surely lead to Joy.

R: That is pleasantly simple advice.

A: All that is required is a grateful acceptance of what mystics have called "The Breath of Life from the Fount of Goodness." Some call this verdant fountain "God" but you should be careful of terms like this because they have become so highly charged over the centuries that they may actually impede your awakening.

R: If I can't turn to the God then who can I turn to?

A: Goodness itself. The term 'God' is the root of the word *Good.* You don't have to anthropomorphize it. Goodness doesn't care what you call it. It is not a name, it is a vibration. Regardless of how you define your Source, this Great Presence is your Redeemer.

Goodness alone is your savior on every plane and dimension.

R: That is liberating. Why would anyone resist such an attractive idea?

A: Because your ego has you convinced that *you must create yourself.* This of course is an immature and even arrogant thought. You don't have enough information to create one hair on your head, let alone construct your whole Being. This task is best left to your Holy Guardian Angel.

The Trap of Circular Thinking

'He drew a circle around the face of the waters and set the boundary of Light and darkness'. - Proverbs 8:27

ometimes it feels like we humans are just chasing our own tails.

.

A: This is circular thinking and it is important to understand if you want to ascend the spiral staircase of Consciousness. You need to understand that you have been trapped in "Flatland." Humans have created a vicious circle of self-perpetuating fear thoughts that have locked them into a flat, two dimensional world of denial.

37

R: Can you give me some examples of these circular fear thoughts?

A: Here is a common fear/circle progression of thoughts:

1. *"Ah ha! Reason tells me that the Devil doesn't exist. I am not a victim. How liberating!"*

2. *"Maybe the Devil does exist but is just trying to get me to believe otherwise so he can deceive me!"*

3. *"I'm afraid to believe the Devil doesn't exist because I don't want to be punished. So I will continue to believe in him just to be safe."*

4. *Circle back to thought #1*

R: And the cycle starts all over again! Do you have another example?

A: Here is a larger cycle from a 'zoomed out' perspective.

Humans generally evolve from:

1. **Bondage to freedom**

2. **Freedom brings awakened spiritual sight.**

3. **Spiritual sight brings courage.**

4. **Courage enables risk.**

5. **Risk brings abundance.**

6. **Abundance brings complacency.**

7. **Complacency leads to apathy.**

8. **Apathy leads to dependency.**

9. **Dependency returns the person back into bondage.**

R: And so, Ouroboros forever circles around feasting on his own tail

A: **Yes and once you understand the two dimensional circular nature of terror you can start to ascend from it. Those used to going around and around in Flatland cannot yet comprehend the freedom of ascending up a spiral into three dimensional (3D) consciousness.**

R: Humanity is starting to awaken to the nature of this higher point of few, isn't it? I know I am.

A: **The end of the Age is bringing quantum awakening to your fledgling mind. There are choirs of space beings singing new waves of Consciousness into existence and heralding the end of these fear cycles for those willing to sing-a-long.**

R: How long do we have to wait for this to happen?

A: **Well, if you were fully awake, you would see that *it has already happened*. Time as you know it doesn't exist from the perspective of higher space. But from a** historical perspective, this awakening is long overdue. After all, it has been six hundred years since you discovered the world isn't flat!

R: Why is it so hard to get off the merry-go-round?

A: These vicious circles create boundaries called 'rings-pass-not' which imprison your consciousness. This cycle is finally broken with penetrating new information from Higher Space.

R: What happens when this information is successfully received?

A: That's when the <u>2D circle appears as a 3D spiral</u> that, rung by rung, gives the mind a ladder leading up and out of Flatland.

R: I understand. Just as a coil viewed from directly above appears as a circle.

A: That's right. A spiral appears only as a circle from directly above it. This is the two dimensional perspective of Flatland.

A slinky coil viewed from the top appears as a 2D circle

A Slinky viewed from a different angle greatly expands the understanding of its shape. Likewise, the higher space version of YOU is infinitely more complex than your familiar 3D version.

A: The Death/Denial circle engenders the same kind of misperception. It exists as a monster lurking in its "dungeon of denial" where it negatively influences your whole life without being seen or questioned.

R: In other words, this Death/Denial circle still functions creatively in the outer world without our knowing it even exists.

A: If you would only open those unused eyes secretly hidden from you in the back of your head, you could see how humans 'project' their idea of death out onto the physical world so that things *appear* to always be dying. Those outer images of death that you project

out then *circle back* to validate the demon still hidden in denial.

R: So this just solidifies the original Fear, making it even stronger.

A: Hence the circle continues cycling forever. Humanity is desperate to find a way out of its dreary 2D world where it endlessly chases its own redundancy. Humans need to 'zoom out' and examine the barrier preventing their freedom into three dimensional viewpoints.

Fourth Dimensional Vision

"Existence is awareness without boundaries."
– Deepak Chopra

ell me more about these exciting new higher space skills like flying, 360 degree vision and omni-directional Awareness.

A: In 4D, you appear to turn yourself inside out! Currently you are accustomed to a 3D unfolding, expanding, "big bang" universe. But, from higher space you have the added perspective that you also live in an IN-folding universe where Time flows in the opposite direction.

R: Time flows backward? That is an intriguing thought.

A: From this point of view, your Life doesn't end in death but <u>begins</u> with it and progresses back through old age while growing increasingly younger until you are reunited with your innocence in the Original Orgasm.

R: Man, I love the sound of that! It's mind boggling!

A: The Heartgasm at the "end" of time will appear when all living things have finally taken on each other's qualities. All relationships will be fulfilled and the Universe will rest in oneness once again until the next fragmentation is perceived and the 'New' Creation is projected. But for now, let's be about exploring what is holding you back from this expanded awareness.

Breaking Through the 'Ring-Pass-Not'

"A breakdown is the beginning of a breakthrough, a trauma that prepares you for a radical transformation." - Cherrie Moraga

 would like to understand the ring-pass-not barrier.

A: The ring-pass-not is not unlike an egg shell that needs to be penetrated from the inside in order for the emerging chick to get out.

R: I looked up 'ring-pass-not' in the Theosophical Glossary. It said:

> "Ring-Pass-Not is a profoundly mystical term signifying the circle or bounds that contain a defined pool of consciousness. "For instance, the ring-pass-not for animals is the inability to experience self-consciousness or self-reflection."

> "For example if a dog is in a room which he desires to leave, he will run to the door he is accustomed to using and will sit there whining for the door to be opened. He knows where the exit is, but the ring-pass-not seals out the self-conscious aspect of his mind required to open the door."

A: This is exactly how it is with humans, only one level up on the evolutionary spiral. *You know where the door is but don't yet know how to open it by yourself.*

R: What is the most obvious ring-pass-not for humanity?

A: It is the barrier that prevents you from having the ability to fly, think yourself places or participate in any of the other gifts that attend fourth dimensional

perspectives. Like a dog waiting for his master to open the door, you must await your Guide to open the gates of Consciousness for you. As always, you need but *ask and you shall receive.*

R: I LOVE the idea of flying so I am determined to get this. In other words, humans live in a closed circle of self-awareness and are not as yet able to step off the circle in order to _use_ their self-awareness effectively.

A: You have a good reason to celebrate because your dream of flying is about to be fulfilled. You are learning about the ring-pass-not and how to penetrate it with the spear of Gratitude.

R: It sounds like there are some exciting new adventures waiting beyond the new frontier of consciousness!

A: Certainly, those willing to stick their heads through that delicate membrane will partake of many new joys in higher space.

R: Alright, here is a bottom line question. What is the fastest most effective way of stepping through this psychological barrier?

A: Just as parents help teach a child how to walk; humans need help learning to navigate the new horizons of Being. Just as walking is a strange skill for the child, flying and thinking yourself places are still strange skills for you. They are difficult at first because other than in your dreams, these abilities lie beyond your comfortably defined world view. The good news is that each person on Earth has been assigned a perfect flight instructor to teach him.

Why am I Here in the First Place?

"You ask if your mission on Earth is finished:
If you're alive, it isn't" – Richard Bach

You call humans "godmonkeys." Is this because we are half animals and half gods?

A: No, it's because you are a god who has retained the element of fear from the animal kingdom. Fear comes from the residual, evolutionary response held over from the mammalian fight or flight impulse. From an angelic perspective this appears as a self-enclosed, semi-conscious state of circular existence. It originates as an unwelcome idea that was reluctantly accepted by humanity. According to some scriptures, this is termed "The Fall of Man."

R: Why in the world did we ever do that?

A: You didn't *want* to accept the idea of death but you did because you believed it. You became so terrified that you pushed it back into denial and have been trying to get rid of this carbuncle from your body of memories ever since. Remember, your soul is the sum total of all the memories you acquired over the ages.

R: I remember well when I first became aware of death. I was just four or five years old when my baby sitter told me that if I didn't behave, I would go to hell when I die. I will never forget the moment that dark, cold intruder first entered my being.

A: As with all humans, this traumatic moment heralds the loss of Original Innocence. From that moment you are a changed person, and not for the better. If you use the experience as a device for awakening, the problem becomes a blessing. Like everyone else, you have spent much of your life playing hide and seek with this demon. By the way, a*nyone who doesn't believe in angels and demons has yet to explain where their thoughts come from.*

R: If death is just "a thought," why can't we just forget about it and move on?

A: While it's true that Death doesn't actually exist, at first you need to approach it as if it does. The wisest among you seek to face and deal with this denied terror in physical Life so that they can 'hit the ground running' when called to make the Great Transition. It's all about creating a joyous death rather than a terrifying, agonizing one.

R: It is said that "The Truth will set you free." Others say, "The Truth hurts." Which is it?

A: Truth "hurts" only when it's resisted. When properly received, Truth is unbelievably and wonderfully liberating. "The Truth shall set you free" is more than just a handy quote. It is a promise from the highest realms! For those who seek to understand the process, *dying becomes not only an ART to be perfected but the most exciting human adventure of all.*

R: I WANT to perfect that art! I want a smooth transition into the next realms. Other than my loved ones, this matters to me more than anything. I'm obsessed with it but don't really know why.

A: Since flying is the accepted mode of travel in your next phase of existence, it makes sense to try out your wings and practice using them so that you may know something of how to navigate the new space when the gates of consciousness open.

R: Fantastic.

A: Yet, this won't happen completely yet because a baby must first be born before it can master the skill of walking.

R: I sure miss the flying dreams I used to have as a child.

A: These dreams are previews of the skills you will enjoy when you find yourself inhabiting your 'Lighter' body.

The Bardos

"Misty meadows...You will find your way" –Moody Blues

riel, if you wouldn't mind, could you please talk about the Tibetan Bardos?

A: Both the ancient Egyptians and the Tibetan Buddhists have documented six states of existence between this life and the next. These are rooms or states of awareness that arise just before, during and right after death. These states are described in depth from a Buddhist perspective in the 'Tibetan Book of the Dead.' (For a brief description of the Bardos, see Appendix B)

R: This sounds complicated. Do we have to totally understand the Bardos in order to have a smooth transition?

A: No. Judeo Christian and other western programs are able to accomplish the same end. These are generally faster methods of transition for impatient westerners. Buddhism is an effective path for the Asian mindset but for most westerners, these Tibetan symbols serve mainly as handy guide posts. Many of

49

the Bardos can be 'leapfrogged' if humans can connect with their Guide and learn to face and transform the denial of death *while still in a physical body*. (See Practicing Dying)

R: So, just facing death correctly is the whole issue, isn't it?

A: You are told, "Hold your friends close but hold your enemies closer." The idea of death should never be allowed to wander too far away.

R: "Carry death on our left shoulder," as Don Juan used to say.

A: Indeed, some courageous adventurers even manage to enter directly the bliss of omnipresent Existence in one single act of Awakening. But to accomplish this leapfrog, they need real motivation diving into their terror and the helping hand of their invisible guide.

Ariel, my Personal Guide

"This Guardian Angel doesn't grant wishes nor sprinkle fairy dust. But rather tells me when I should, when I shouldn't and when I must."
- Mandy Salter

Ariel you call yourself an "inter-dimensional midwife." Is that your only function as my HGA?

A: I simply help tease the frightened, cowering aspects of yourself out of denial and into the healing Light of Awareness. Everyone has an Inner Guide making suggestions to them all through their lives but unlike you, most people don't realize it yet. Usually it's not until their last days on Earth that their Holy Guardian Angel appears. The reason for this is that everyone's guide speaks to them through the software of *their own thoughts and feelings*. Therefore most people simply confuse this important conversation with mere inner dialog. *At first they think they are just talking to themselves. So* they ignore or cut off the conversation before it even starts.

R: So the main lesson for humans is to distinguish their own thoughts from the impulses of their inner guide.

A: Again, the best way for a man or woman to contact their HGA is the same way you did. Simply ASK! And there are devices to help speed up the process as well.

Recognizing Your Own Guide

*"My Angel, My Conscience, My Inner Voice
With me from the Beginning, Guiding every Choice.* - A

ou mentioned that humanity has many different

names and faces for their different guides.

- **A: Humanity's invisible helpers are as unique to each person as their finger prints are. Depending upon your ability to receive, they can appear as a demigod in a cloud of Light, or a simple leaf flapping in the wind, or a pair of "knothole eyes" staring back at you from the oak tree in your back yard.** *For some it may even be their departed mother or uncle.*

- **To Christians he may appear as** *Jesus.*

- **To New Agers, the** *Inner Voice.*

- **To Magicians, it is the** *HGA or Holy Guardian Angel*

- **Humanists call it** *Higher Conscience.*

- **To American Indians,** *The Great Spirit.*

- **The Marians call her** *Mary*

- **To the Hawaiians it is** *Aumakua*,

- **The Taoist simply call it** *"TAO,"* **the Flow and voice of Harmony or The Music of the Spheres.**

- **To Buddhists, it is Emptiness, or The Void (Nirvana)**

Divine Love will use any means available to reach you. Again, it only matters that you RECOGNIZE its presence so you can partake of its flawless guidance amidst the chaos inundating your world.

R: Most people haven't discovered their Guide yet.

A: It's not easy for many people to recognize their HGA because it speaks with a SINGLE voice whereas the

voices of fear, while rooted in the *single* thought of death, are *legion* and jump around like a bus filled with drunken monkeys."

The Contact Procedure
Harmonic Resonance with your Invisible Guide

"There's a part of you that seems to hide,
It may be loaded with worry, fear and pride.
Be still, in this moment, bring your attention inside.
Allow that Voice to be your one guide. "

- Shifu Ahles

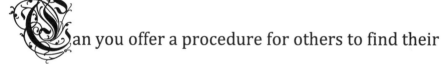an you offer a procedure for others to find their HGA?

A: Try this device:

The next time you have a particularly inspiring thought, immediately stop your world and ask that thought (just as if you were talking to a person in front of you) "Where did you come from? Who are you?" Then wait for the response. Eventually your thoughts will seem to start answering back.

At first you will think you are just talking to yourself (which on one level is true) but don't be fooled.

Persevere in this conversation with your so called "imaginary friend" until you feel the presence of a protective energy.

From this point you are connected and may even strike up a conversational friendship with your Holy Guardian Angel.

Eventually, you will find this Being to be quite literally your Redeemer. Your Holy Guardian Angel is nothing less than the Holy Spirit, condensed into an invisible yet recognizable focus of individualized intelligence. Your personal HGA exists solely for your own protection and guidance.

As your guide becomes more and more of an established part of your being, your outer teachers, including writings like this book, will become less and less important.

For those who aren't sure whether or not they have connected with their HGA, it's good to repeat one thing: <u>*Everyone* has an HGA and everyone hears and follows it but most don't even know it.</u>

Helping Others Through the Veil
"Friend take my hand. Together we'll explore the Promised Land" –A

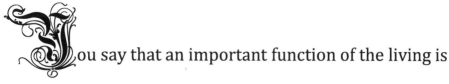ou say that an important function of the living is to help the dying across the great divide. How can we best learn to do that?

A: Let's start with the simpler process of helping a pet (like the family dog or cat) pass through the Veil.

Being the compassionate beings that most humans are, you often like to spare your animal friends unnecessary suffering by having them put peacefully to sleep. Humans should be so lucky to have this option!

R: Believe it or not, I am more terrified of my dogs dying than myself.

A: If and when you are in the position of helping your animals pass over and if you are willing to face your own depths, you can help catapult your animal friends into a wonderful state of existence. This may be done by holding your dear pet in your arms as the vet administers the euthanizing agent. In your mind and heart, say to him "It's time for you to re-enter the Peace from whence you came and from where I first created you. When I look at you I am not seeing a body but only my own precious Love projected out onto my movie screen of Creation."

R: I still haven't fully grasped the idea that I "create" my own pets.

A: To totally understand that humans actually help construct their movie (world) by *projecting* awareness outward through the film of their held beliefs is a bit beyond the scope of this conversation. This topic is

covered in depth in the second book, 'All Things are Possible.' In this book however, let's stay with the task of liberating your Spirit from its prison of the fear of death.

R: OK. Please continue.

A: If you are able to see your pet as your own creation, it allows both of you to experience and share Divine Love from totally different angles than previously thought possible. Say to your departing friend, "My dear little friend, you are a unique version of my Holy Love in one of its endless facets. Thank you for sharing your short life with me."

R: That is intensely moving.

A: This kind of projection is how all living things are made to appear "out there" in the objective world.

R: You have mentioned before that our eyes are projectors, not just receptors.

A: That is an important point to remember. Just as humans are the projections of their Higher Angels, you also project living beings to inhabit the screen of your Creation. You are baby gods, remember?

R: How about helping our *human* friends cross over?

A: There is no work more important for humans than to show a person how to access *their own* HGA before they pass over. The sooner this can be done the better. This may be done by talking with them during the transition or reading inspired passages from books like the Tibetan Book of the Dead. (See Appendix C)

As an acting guide, you should gently suggest that he listen for (and try to imagine) his own Angel. This is best done before he totally leaves the Physical Plane but it can even be successful for up to three days *after* clinical death. The sooner this can happen, the smoother your friend's departure may be.

R: I wish I would have known this information to help my parents when they died.

A: Your parents had help I assure you. All these things happen at the time they are supposed to. When the dying have finally made their connection with their HGA, nothing else needs to be done by you. From that point they should just let go and follow him into the Light. One need not worry about anything like watching for the Bardos, fighting off demons or anything else. The HGA has the single function of protecting his assignment!

R: That is really comforting. What if a dying friend hasn't yet connected with his HGA?

A: He she can still be greatly helped by a soothing voice reading inspiring passages. He will wind up in the most appropriate place for his level of awakening anyway. He will be surrounded by infinite Mercy. He just won't be as aware of what's happening to him as someone who dies consciously.

R: It would be nice if I could help as much as possible.

A: You can also swiftly create a smooth transition by unselfishly *taking on* the denied fear of your dying friend. This is easy for a guide who knows what he is doing because he has already learned to find and easily transform those repressed engrams within himself.

R: What if the person I'm helping lacks faith in the spiritual world?

A: Then your work becomes more difficult but still helpful. Many wrestle with their lack of faith during this transition but *your* courage as a guide will ease their angst and make it possible for them to make great strides toward their Liberation.

R: OK, here comes the hardest one for me. How can we best help deliver our mates and closest family members?

A: To truly be effective in this, one must understand the nature of all close relationships. If you marry someone or find a deep bond with another it is because they have qualities you are attracted to and likewise, you have qualities attractive to them. More importantly, they have aspects of their nature *that you need to absorb* in order to become more of what you are and therefore become more whole.

R: This is a hidden Truth that everyone could benefit from.

A: The hidden truth is this: People in close relationships actually *become* each other. You have noticed how couples that have been together for many years talk the same way and walk together in locked cadence. It is because they have actually *turned into each other* and have taken on each other's essence. Both people are now more complete because they not only have become more of themselves, but they have become more of each other as well.

R: Great. "The whole has become greater than the sum of its parts."

A: Likewise, you may have noticed how people even begin to look like their pets after a time and vice

versa. Knowing this, you can see how the death of a close relationship is quite impossible. Consider the division of a one celled animal like the amoeba that splits itself into two halves. If one of the halves dies, the other is not reduced because of it. No not at all. It contains everything the other half had.

Similarly, if you have a close loved who one departs, he or she *has left their essence in you where it will reside for all Eternity*. Never forget the larger picture here. Relationships exist so that we may all eventually *become* each other. At that point, "God will have wholly discovered Himself." Both Creator and Creation will rest until the next cycle of exploratory fragmentation dawns.

Finally, the Awareness!

"And so I cross into another world shyly waiting for an invitation from that unknown realm that I would trespass on." - D. H. Lawrence

know you don't like calling it "heaven" but can you further elaborate on the nature of this state anyway?

A: You know already that it can't be explained. A 3D mind cannot comprehend 4D reality. Let alone the fifth, sixth and seventh dimensions. Geometric symbols and mathematics are the only way to discuss

higher Space. They are far better than words to accurately describe the gift of Heaven. (See Appendix E)

R: Well, what about poetry?

A: Poetry is every bit as effective as geometry in explaining Higher Space. Only music is higher. But this particular work is intended to give a symbolic, <u>conceptual</u> map of the landscape for those who need to understand intellectually.

R: Eventually, both Head and Heart are supposed to work together in our experience of Higher Space, correct?

A: That's right. Heaven is the Marriage of Ecstatic Love and Perfect Peace Profound. The start of Genesis, "In the Beginning was the Word," is not nearly as descriptive as it could be.

R: Maybe it would be more accurate to say "In the beginning was The Tone? Or maybe even, "In the Beginning was the Word AND the Tone."

A: "In the beginning was the........... SONG!"

"...and the last enemy to be abolished is death." -1 Corinthians 1

Appendix A:
The 5 Stages of Grief

Dr. Elisabeth Kubler Ross, in her seminal book "*On Death and Dying*" has done significant research and endless interviews with hundreds of dying people and found there is a sequence everyone goes through during their deathbed transition from Life to the afterlife. These five Stages of Grief occur in the following order:

1. Denial—"This can't be happening, not to me."

2. Anger _"Why me? It's not fair!" "How can this happen to me? God, you are to blame."

3. Bargaining— "I'll be good, God. Just let me live long enough to see my children graduate." "I'll do anything for a few more years." "I would give my life savings if I could only..."

4. Depression— "I'm so sad, why bother with anything?" "It's hopeless. I'm going to die so what's the point?" "Why go on?

5. Acceptance— "I'm dying, I can't fight it, I may as well prepare for it and glean what I can from it."

A: In this last stage, the individual begins to come to terms with her/his mortality or that of a loved one. This is usually when the HGA (Holy Guardian Angel) appears to those who haven't made the connection yet.

Since everyone starts to die from the moment they are born this Kubler Ross model roughly follows the Tibetan Bardos and works for the various stages of your *earthly* existence, too. Roughly stated, with exceptions, these stages also appear in order from cradle to grave in almost everyone. The following timeline is typical.

1. **Denial**. When you are teenagers you feel immortal. You deny your human weaknesses and the future seems very bright...until you get glimpses of the fact that you are all doomed to "fail" in the end. This recognition brings about:

2. **Anger**. This is the syndrome of the "angry young man" in his twenties. Those in their 20s and early 30s tend to be uncomfortable and prickly toward life in general because their "immortality" has been challenged.

3. **Bargaining** is the next stage. The late 30s and 40s bring about the first conscious recognition of the processes that define your mortality. You bargain with God and promise to get busy 'being good' by working harder and fulfilling your familial responsibilities. "Dammit, if I'm gonna die I at least want to go to heaven"

4. **Depression** in the face of certain entropy starts to appear in the 40s and early 50s. This is when you search every nook and cranny for the solution to the speedy encroachment of your demise.

5. **Acceptance** is the final stage of grief. This is why the golden years become so peaceful for many. (Especially for those who have nurtured their spiritual life).

Appendix B:
The Bardos

The Six Stages of Life and Death as documented by Tibetan Buddhism

1. The *Shin-ay Bardo*, is the ever present state of Awareness in Physical Life. This is your familiar workaday state of consciousness from conception until the last breath.

2. The *Milam Bardo* or Astral world of dreams is the awareness of the finer, less dense just above the Physical. This is where you learn to fly and gather your treasures in Heaven by way of your *Imagination*.

3. The *Samten Bardo* is the Bardo of stillness. This is the quiet world visited most often by meditators and the advanced seekers of silence while still in physical existence.

4. The *Chikkhai Bardo* is the brilliant luminous world which appears precisely at the moment of Death. This is the familiar "Light at the end of the tunnel" experienced by many at the time of their transition.

5. *The Chönyid Bardo* is the first experience of unconditioned Truth or reality for the traveler. This is the soul's re-introduction to its true nature. (Dharmata)

6. The *Sidpa Bardo* is the first experience of actually BECOMING that oneness or ultimate Existence. This is the state of existence which is beyond all manifestation. It is the capstone of the pyramid of consciousness. In the language of Qabala it is the crowning sphere called 'Kether'.

Readings For The Dying

*To be read with a soothing voice by a guide seeking
to help a loved one passing through the portal of death.*

Khalil Gibran

"…Trust the dreams, for in them is hidden the gate to eternity.

Your fear of death is but the trembling of the shepherd when he stands before the king whose hand is to be laid upon him in honor.

Is the shepherd not joyful beneath his trembling, that he shall wear the mark of the king?

Yet is he not more mindful of his trembling?

For what is it to die but to stand naked in the wind and to melt into the sun?

And what is it to cease breathing, but to free the breath from its restless tides that it may rise and expand and seek God unencumbered?

Only when you drink from the river of silence shall you indeed sing.

And when you have reached the mountain top, then you shall begin to climb.

And when the earth shall claim your limbs, then shall you truly dance."

The Tibetan Book of the Dead- Reading #1

"Now when the Bardo of dying dawns upon me,

I will abandon all grasping, yearning and attachment,

Enter undistracted into a clear awareness of the teaching,

And eject my consciousness into the space of unborn awareness;

As I leave this compound body of flesh and blood

I will know it to be a transitory illusion."

Thomas Merton

"I have no idea where I am going

I do not see the road ahead of me. I cannot know for certain where it will end.

Nor do I really know myself, and the fact that I think I am following your will does not mean that I am actually doing so.

But I believe that the desire to please you does in fact please you.

And I hope that I have that desire in all that I am doing.

And I know that if I do this, you will lead me by the right road though I may know nothing about it.

Therefore will I trust you always though I may seem to be lost

and in the shadow of death, I will not fear, for you are ever with me and you will never leave me to face my perils alone.

"Through your blessing, grace, and guidance,

through the power of the Light that streams from you:

May all my negative karma, destructive emotions,

obscurations and blockages be purified and removed,

May I know myself forgiven

for all the harm I may have thought and done,

May I accomplish this profound practice of phowa, (transferring consciousness)

and die a good and peaceful death,

And through the triumph of my death,

may I be able to benefit all other beings, living or dead."

Psalm 23

"The Lord is my shepherd; I shall not want.

He maketh me to lie down in green pastures:

he leadeth me beside the still waters.

He restoreth my soul:

He leadeth me in the paths of righteousness for his name's sake.

Yea, though I walk through the valley of the shadow of death; I will fear no evil: for thou art with me; thy rod and thy staff they comfort me.

Thou preparest a table before me in the presence of mine enemies: thou anointest my head with oil; my cup runneth over.

Surely goodness and mercy shall follow me all the days of my life; and I will dwell in the house of the Lord forever."

Mary Elizabeth Frye

"Do not stand at my grave and weep

I am not there. I do not sleep.

I am a thousand winds that blow.

I am the diamond glints on snow.

I am the sunLight on ripened grain.

I am the gentle autumn rain.

When you awaken in the morning's hush,

I am the swift uplifting rush

Of quiet birds in circled fLight.

I am the soft stars that shine at night.

Do not stand at my grave and cry.

I am not there. I did not die."

"When my time has come and impermanence and death have caught up with me,

When the breath ceases, and the body and mind go their separate ways,

May I not experience delusion, attachment, and clinging, But remain in the natural state of ultimate reality."

Geometric Aids

The inter-dimensional world of squares and orbs.

R: Turning to those higher perspectives, you said once that a 3D sphere becomes a 4D hypersphere once it is turned inside out. That is an interesting thought but a tough one to visualize.

A: Yes, a 4D hypersphere may be thought of as a 3D sphere unfolded and turned inside out. <u>Likewise your 4D body is your 3D body unfolded and turned inside out.</u>

R: I can't yet visualize my 4D body. I get glimpses of what you are saying but this topic still seems quite cryptic. But I'm starting to see just how powerful these geometric devices are.

A: You have made a lot of progress transcending the limitations of two dimensional worlds.

R: Is 2D awareness becoming obsolete.

A: No, all the dimensions are to be understood and used, each in its appropriate place. For instance it is easier to eat your dinner off of a 2D plate than a 3D basketball.

R: So we only need to release the <u>limitations</u> of each plane. Then we are free to use it instead of being imprisoned behind its rings-pass-not.

A: You don't have to give up circles just because you have discovered spirals. Here are some symbols that show the progression of a straight line evolving from 1D to 4D.

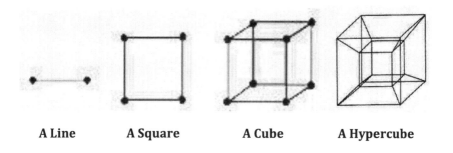

| A Line | A Square | A Cube | A Hypercube |

Not that each new dimension appears at a RIGHT ANGLE to each previous dimension. Likewise, Heaven exists at a right angle to your 3D world of height, width and depth.

Here is another geometric analogy way of seeing this progression is by contemplation evolution of the square into the *hypercube*:

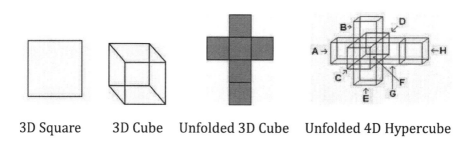

3D Square   3D Cube   Unfolded 3D Cube   Unfolded 4D Hypercube

By analogy,

1. A One Dimensional Being can move forward in a straight line
2. A 2D Being has learned the added ability to turn corners
3. A 3D Being has added DEPTH to his world and is able to *delve into things*
4. A Four Dimensional Being has mastered the direction of TIME and is even able to reverse it. He has also mastered space so he is able to fly.

A 4D Being is one who has finally learned all he can from 3D reality and has penetrated the ring-pass-not and mastered TIME as well as SPACE. He has in essence turned himself inside out and is able to *think* himself places. Such is the joyful once and Future Home of dear Humanity.

Appendix E:
Who Is Ariel?
From the Preface of the book, 'All Things are Possible'

On one level, Ariel is an aspect of myself; an imaginary friend that I created and imbued with infinite wisdom.

The social revolutions in the middle of the last century created in me a life changing spiritual event that rendered every day peace of mind quite impossible. I was driven to become an ambassador of the Love generation. With a natural love of psycho-drama and comedy (I was always the ham) I had a seamstress make a wizard costume for me and proceeded to create a character I called "The Wizard of Harmony."

At first the costume was merely the garish prop of a street musician. It was a semi-joke. Strangely however, as I wore the new robe with stars and moons at concerts and folk fairs, something inexplicable started to happen.

When I first wore the costume, most people just laughed at me while others seemed to look right through me as if I were invisible. I later attributed this invisibility to the cognitive dissonance created by the audacity of some guy pretending to have magical powers. This later proved to become an effective device that led to the remembrance of invisibility as a lost magical art!

Interestingly, a few people would actually suspend disbelief long enough to walk up and ask "the wizard" to give them advice in solving their personal problems.

Miraculously, I often succeeded! I not only seemed to have the right solutions for these complete strangers but often appeared to know what their problems were before they even asked.

They were amazed and so was I. It was a psychic anomaly that started to create notoriety in the Lifestyle sections of local newspapers and Oregon university campuses.

This voice that came from me wasn't *really* me, or was it!? It was a stern voice that came from inside me yet beyond me; a compassionate, intelligent and yet edgy voice that occasionally frightened but always intrigued bystanders including myself.

Wanting to see the full possibilities of this phenomenon and to the dismay of family and friends who thought I was possessed, I decided to exploit it. I even made a five inch square sign to wear around my neck:

WIZARD
of
HARMONY

FREE, ANY PROBLEM SOLVED
(Inquire Within)

My folks and friends have always considered me eccentric but now they became frightened that I was downright schizoid. Regardless of the overt and covert murmuring, a growing number of people were actually starting to believe there might be something authentic about this spooky guy so they secretly sought out the Wizard for advice.

By 1970 as a wandering vagabond owning nothing but a duffle bag and guitar, most of my time was spent singing on the street using tools like the Tarot, Bible and I-Ching to give spiritual and psychic readings. Many were becoming increasingly amazed at the psychic accuracy of this strange young man wearing the garment and mantle of a Wizard.

As I grew less self-conscious, a larger and more serious entity emerged inside the costume. This was when the spiritual "roto-rooter" who likes to call himself *"Ariel"* made himself known to me.

I allowed this emergence because I was starting to suspect that Ariel was something quite profound. It was becoming increasingly apparent that he was what Ralph Waldo Emerson called my "over soul" or a higher aspect of myself.

I'm still not convinced of this but regardless, this larger 'me' seemed unfettered with the addictions and trappings of my life and expressed a spiritual equilibrium I had heretofore not experienced.

That was nearly 50 years ago. As of this writing Ariel is still with me. When I asked why he would use such a predictable handle he replied, "Because it's my name."

Ariel is what the Hermetic Magicians of old would call a "telesmic image," which may be defined as: *"the held and nurtured mental picture of what one would like to become."* Sort of like a spiritual "business plan," if you will.

I have since learned that this phenomenon is not peculiar to me. It portends the universal destiny of all who seek to become better humans. The principle is simply this: WHAT ONE INTENDS WITHOUT DOUBT HAPPENS! Or said another way, WHATEVER ONE DESIRES TO BECOME,

ONE BECOMES, no matter how unorthodox or ridiculous the desire may be. The one rule required is not to *reverse* or negate the process with self-doubt and/or the collective doubt of others.

The masters and magicians of ancient times were familiar with a kind of creativity that allowed them to focus their intent to a point of even *creating living beings*! I'm not sure if this is where Ariel comes from, but I suspect it is. All I know is, as I said before, for me, Ariel is real.

Ron Lloyd - July 1971

April, 2012